T0007992

My Dear Friend,

We have traveled all around the world and met many wonderful children. Unfortunately, we cannot meet everyone, so we wanted to say hello and share this story with you. We wrote this book to help you remember that even when you are having a hard time, joy is never far away.

Sometimes we get sad. Sometimes we get angry. Sometimes we get scared. But after the rain and the storms, we have found there is often a rainbow.

We hope you will find joy (and rainbows) in the pages of this book and that you can share this joy with the people you love. This is the secret of joy we discovered together—the more joy we share, the more joy we have.

With love, your friends,

**His Holiness the Dalai Lama**

**Archbishop Desmond Tutu**

His Holiness the Dalai Lama & Archbishop Desmond Tutu

# THE LITTLE BOOK OF JOY

with Douglas Abrams and Rachel Neumann

Illustrated by
Rafael López

Crown Books for Young Readers
New York

One of us grew up in a little house.

One of us grew up in a big house.

Our houses were

on opposite sides
of the world.

Often we were sad. And lonely.

Both of us wished for a friend.

Sometimes the other kids
wouldn't let us play.

Or they were very far away.

We wondered if we would always be sad and lonely.

But when we sat still and
breathed in the quiet,

we noticed something beautiful.

If you just focus on the thing that is making you sad, then the sadness is all you see.

But if you look around, you will see that joy is everywhere.

Joy is the warm tingly feeling of the
sun tickling your toes in the morning.

It's the giggly, squiggly feeling when you are doing something silly.

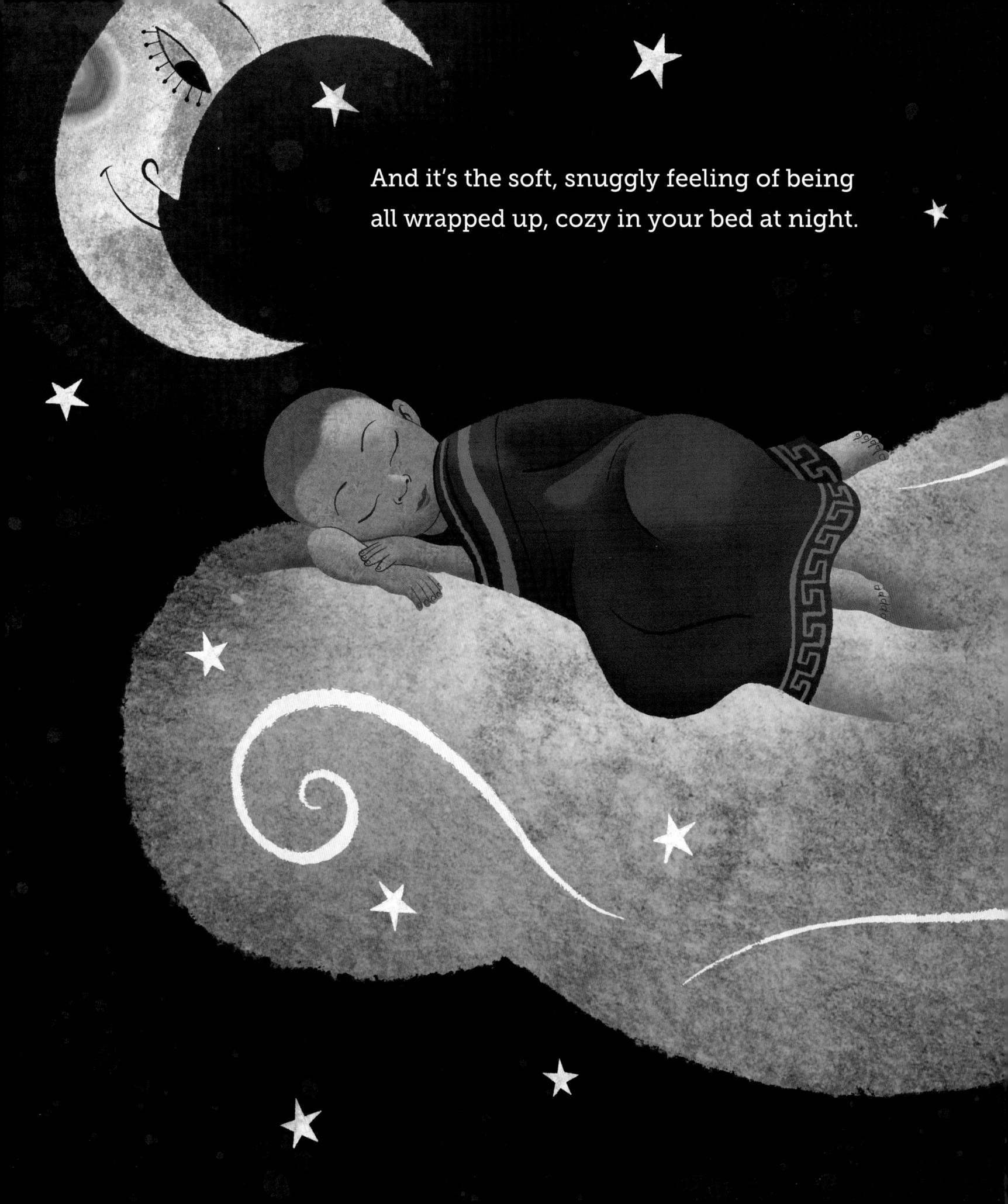

And it's the soft, snuggly feeling of being all wrapped up, cozy in your bed at night.

Even when you are caught in the rain
and your joy is washed away, it's waiting
at the bottom of the puddle.

Even if you slam the door and your joy can't get in, it's just on the other side waiting in a loving hug.

And even if there is a loud noise in the night and your joy gets scared away, it comes streaming right back with the light of the silvery moon.

Joy is the bubbly, bouncy
feeling of finding a good friend.

And once you let joy in, like magic,
your heart always has room for more.

We discovered that the more joy
we shared, the more joy we had.

And the more joy we had,
the more joy we could share.

So look for the joy all around you . . .
and share it!
Write it in a letter.
Play it on a drum.
88 39

Sing it to the sky.

It will travel.

Up in the air.

Across the ocean.

Someone will find it . . .

親愛なる友人

. . . and share it. And as it spreads from person to person, the world will fill with **JOY**.

Miranda Penn Turin

**His Holiness the 14th Dalai Lama, Tenzin Gyatso,** is the spiritual leader of the Tibetan people and of Tibetan Buddhism. He was awarded the Nobel Peace Prize in 1989 and the US Congressional Gold Medal in 2007. The Dalai Lama has traveled the world to promote kindness and compassion, interfaith understanding, protection of Tibetan culture, respect for the environment, and, above all, deeper human values based on a sense of the oneness of humanity, with the aim of creating a more compassionate society. He has lived in exile in Dharamsala, India, since 1959.

**Desmond Mpilo Tutu, Archbishop Emeritus of Southern Africa,** was a prominent leader in the crusade for justice and reconciliation in South Africa. He was awarded the Nobel Peace Prize in 1984 and the Presidential Medal of Freedom in 2009. After South Africa's transition to democracy in 1994, he was appointed chair of the Truth and Reconciliation Commission, where he pioneered a new way for countries to move forward after experiencing civil conflict and oppression. Archbishop Tutu was regarded as a leading moral voice and an icon of hope.

To the children of the world
—His Holiness the Dalai Lama and Archbishop Desmond Tutu

To all who walk the path of peace
—R.L.

Text copyright © 2022 by His Holiness the Dalai Lama and Archbishop Desmond Tutu
Jacket art and interior illustrations copyright © 2022 by Rafael López

All rights reserved. Published in the United States by Crown Books for Young Readers, an imprint of Random House Children's Books, a division of Penguin Random House LLC, New York.

Crown and the colophon are registered trademarks of Penguin Random House LLC.

Visit us on the Web! rhcbooks.com

Educators and librarians, for a variety of teaching tools, visit us at RHTeachersLibrarians.com

Library of Congress Cataloging-in-Publication Data is available upon request.
ISBN 978-0-593-48423-4 (hardcover) | ISBN 978-0-593-48424-1 (lib. bdg.) |
ISBN 978-0-593-48425-8 (ebook)

The text of this book is set in 16-point Museo Slab.
The illustrations in this book were created using acrylic, watercolor, pencil, ink, and digital media.
Book design by Jan Gerardi

MANUFACTURED IN ITALY
10 9 8 7 6 5 4 3 2 1
First Edition

Random House Children's Books supports the First Amendment and celebrates the right to read.

Penguin Random House LLC supports copyright. Copyright fuels creativity, encourages diverse voices, promotes free speech, and creates a vibrant culture. Thank you for buying an authorized edition of this book and for complying with copyright laws by not reproducing, scanning, or distributing any part in any form without permission. You are supporting writers and allowing Penguin Random House to publish books for every reader.